# FOR GUITAR

## by Ralph Agresta

The original just got better!
Full-band backup to 10 extended jams in authentic
jazz styles. Includes tips on scales and techniques to use
with each track. In standard notation and tablature.

Cover instruments owned by Scot Arch
Photographed by William H. Draffen
The Washburn guitar appears courtesy of Washburn International

Order No. AM 943118
US International Standard Book Number: 0.8256.1606.9
UK International Standard Book Number: 0.7119.6475.0

Exclusive Distributors:
**Music Sales Corporation**
257 Park Avenue South, New York, NY 10010 USA
**Music Sales Limited**
8/9 Frith Street, London W1V 5TZ England
**Music Sales Pty. Limited**
120 Rothschild Street, Rosebery, Sydney, NSW 2018, Australia

Printed in the United States of America by
Vicks Lithograph and Printing Corporation

**Amsco Publications**
New York/London/Sydney

# CD Track Listing

1. Tuning
2. Be Bop Blues
3. Minor Blues
4. Rhythm Changes
5. Latin Groove
6. Bossa/Samba
7. 32-Bar Swing
8. TV Funk
9. Half Time Shuffle
10. Pop Funk
11. Slow Ballad

# Table of Contents

# Introduction

Hi, I'm Ralph Agresta. Once again, I've invited a few of my musician friends over for an impromptu jazz jam, and as usual, we left room for you to play the solos.

Join me and the rest of your "portable rhythm section," bassist John Abbey, drummer Phil Cimino, and keyboardist Greg Schleiche, as we play through ten of the more common styles found in jazz.

As with the other CDs and books in the *Jamtrax* series, the music here is arranged to cover a wide variety of tempos, keys, and rhythms to provide you, the soloist, with a convenient practice tool that simulates the experience of soloing with a live band.

In this book, you will find the chord charts that lead you through each arrangement as well as several scales and patterns with which you might want to experiment.

I'm sure you will find this a fun way to stretch your musical imagination and to try out new soloing ideas in the privacy of your own room. You may also wish to use the CD to warm up before gigs!

Again, have fun, and I sincerely hope you enjoy and learn from this book and CD.

Ralph Agresta

# Be Bop Blues in B♭

A common scale used by many jazz soloists is this form of the blues scale, which includes the major third (D♮) and the flatted fifth (F♭). Tablature is provided for guitarists.

Here's the same scale up one octave.

The F melodic minor scale will work well in measure 4

The mixolydian scale (which works nicely over dominant chords) can be thought of as a major scale with a flatted seventh. In this case, the E♭ mixolydian scale can be used over the E♭9 chords in the second and fifth measures.

Here the E♭ mixolydian scale is written in two octaves. The first octave has been repositioned for guitarists (check the tablature).

## Chords for "Be Bop Blues"

V = fret number
x = don't play string

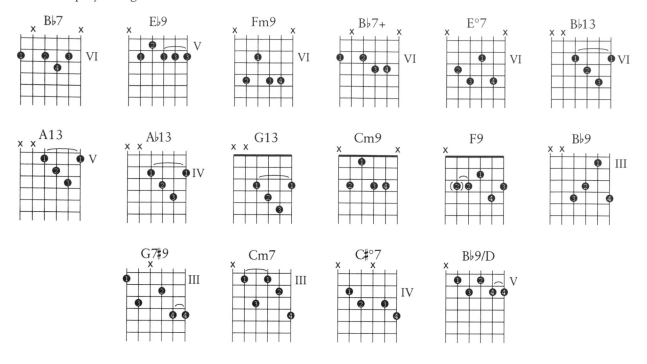

## Be Bop Blues

**Brisk shuffle**

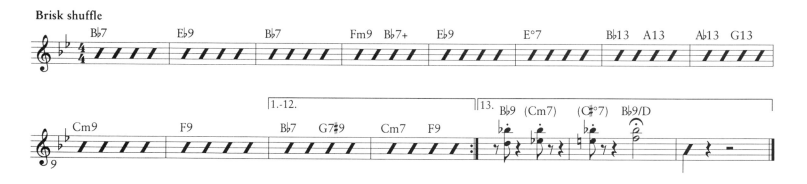

# Minor Blues in C Minor

You'll notice that in the B section of this piece the bass begins to "walk" through the changes, creating a completely different feel from the one in the A section.

The C minor pentatonic scale is probably the simplest scale to use for soloing over these chord changes.

The C melodic minor scale will work equally well here.

Again, you may want to use an F melodic minor scale for playing over the Fm9 chords. This example is in a lower octave and offers a different fingering for guitarists.

The application of the next scale offers an important insight on how to achieve an authentic jazz sound over an altered dominant chord.

Play a melodic minor scale a half step up from the dominant chord. This will give you all the altered tones (♭5, ♯5, ♭9, ♯9) as well as the root, third, and flatted seventh.

Try playing the A♭ melodic minor scale over the G7+ chord.

The A♭ minor (major7) arpeggio (taken from this scale) sounds great over G7+.

## Chords for "Minor Blues"

V = fret number
x = don't play string

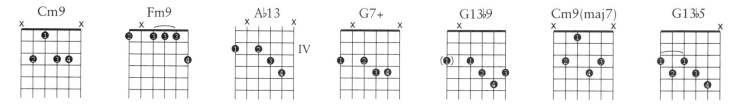

## Minor Blues

Medium shuffle feel

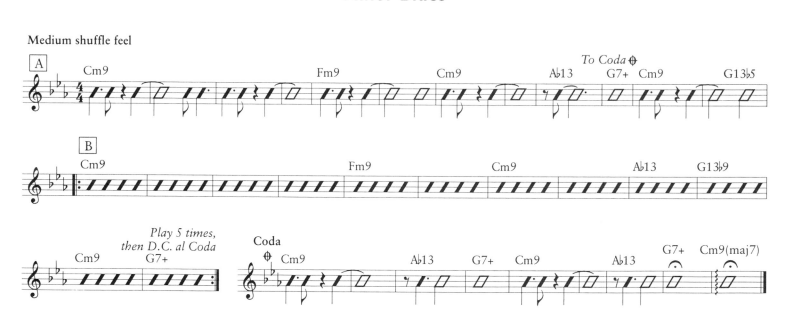

# Rhythm Changes in B♭

The B♭ major pentatonic scale can be used for the [A] sections of "Rhythm Changes."

Another approach you can take is to play short arpeggios over each chord. This will help your technique immensely, as well as your ability to improvise over changes.

Using this idea, here's a lick that works well over measures 3–4, 11–12, and 27–28

Mixolydian scales will sound good over the dominant chords in the [B] section. Here you see D mixolydian, which you would use over the D13 chord.

## Chords for "Rhythm Changes"

V = fret number
x = don't play string

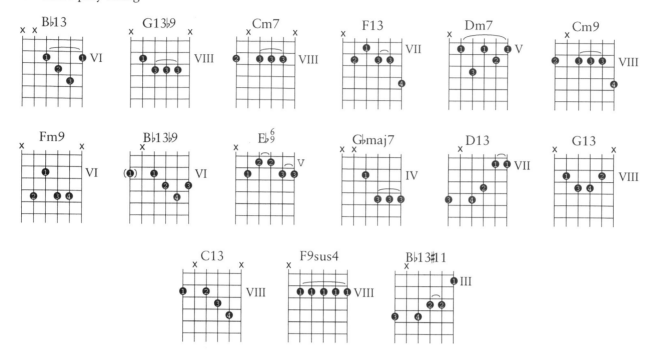

## Rhythm Changes

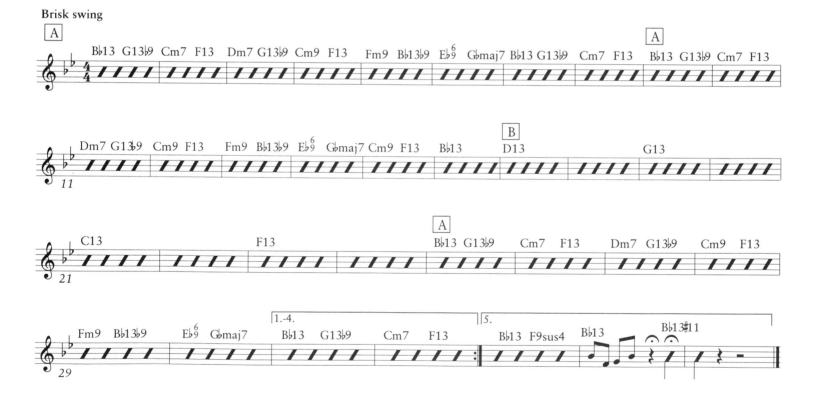

# Latin Groove in C

These three forms of the C major pentatonic scale will work well over the
changes of "Latin Groove." The E♭ note (which functions as the flatted third) is
added to the scale to give it a bluesy sound.

## *Chords for "Latin Groove"*

V = fret number
x = don't play string

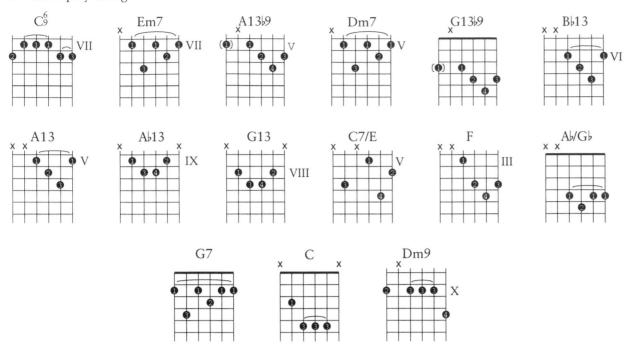

## Latin Groove

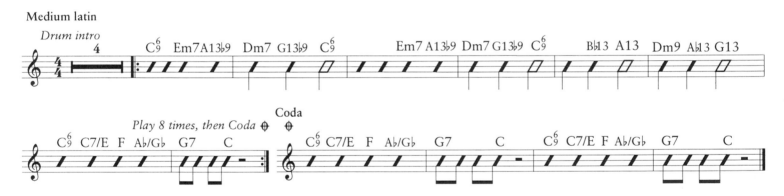

# Bossa/Samba in C Minor

Again we find ourselves in the key of C minor, so refer to the scales and ideas that we used for "Minor Blues."

In measures 13-16 and 29-32, the key modulates to D♭.
The D♭ major scale will work nicely in this section.

Here's a look at a C melodic minor scale that is one octave up from the one we saw in "Minor Blues."

Here's another C minor pentatonic scale.

And here's another F melodic minor scale.

## *Chords for "Bossa/Samba"*

V = fret number
x = don't play string

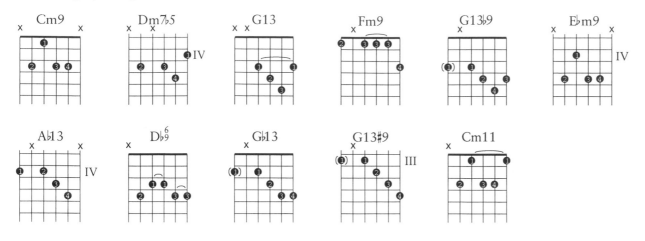

## Bossa/Samba

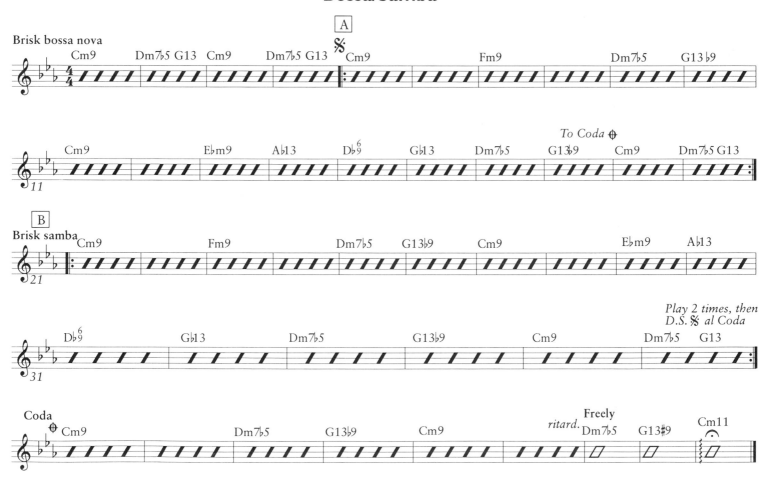

# 32-Bar Swing in E Minor

For "32-Bar Swing," you can use some of the scale applications and ideas mentioned earlier, such as playing the melodic minor scale over minor chords and the mixolydian scale over dominant chords.

Another scale you can play over dominant chords is the half/whole diminished scale, constructed by alternating half steps and whole steps starting from the root.

This one will work over B13♭9.

## *Chords for "32-Bar Swing"*

V = fret number
x = don't play string

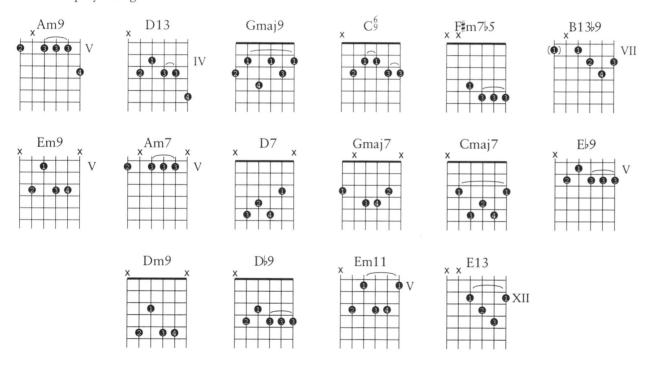

# 32-Bar Swing

Medium swing

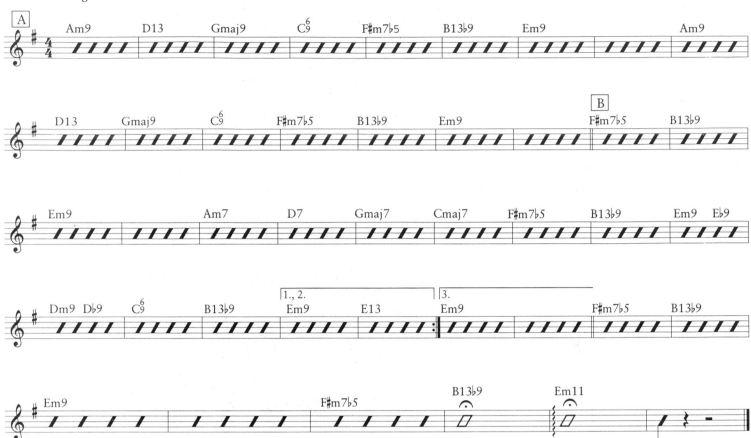

# TV Funk in A

The chord progression in "TV Funk" is a subtle variation on the common I-IV-V progression often found in traditional blues, so it makes sense to use the simple blues and minor pentatonic scales that are usually associated with this style.

This is a two-octave descending A blues scale. Notice that it begins with the flatted third (C).

And here's yet another way of playing the A minor pentatonic scale

Here is a neat riff that is played by adding a flatted fifth (E♭) to an A dorian scale.

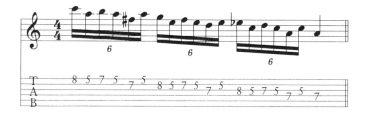

## *Chords for "TV Funk"*

V = fret number
x = don't play string

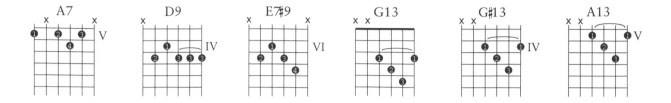

# TV Funk

# Half Time Shuffle in C

In a tune like "Half Time Shuffle" where you're basically playing over one chord (C7♯5♯9), an interesting approach can be taken. Play both the C minor pentatonic and the C♯minor pentatonic scales over the C7♯5♯ 9 chord. This produces a somewhat dissonant, or "outside," sound and adds movement to a static harmony.

This is the Cm pentatonic scale.

And this is the C♯m pentatonic scale.

## Chords for "Half Time Shuffle"

V = fret number
x = don't play string

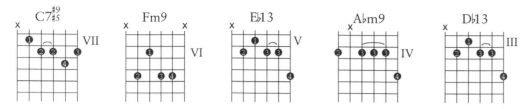

# Half Time Shuffle

Medium shuffle

# Pop Funk in E Minor

The E aeolian scale (which can be thought of as a G major scale) will work well in this situation.

Here are two fingerings for guitar players

Try using the A mixolydian scale for the [B] sections that begin at measures 9 and 25.

## *Chords for "Pop Funk"*

V = fret number
x = don't play string.

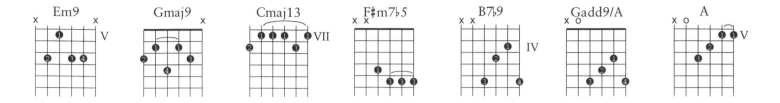

## Pop Funk

# Slow Ballad in F Minor

The [A] section of "Slow Ballad" can be treated as a simple minor blues. Use the F minor pentatonic scale – you'll be surprised at how well this simple scale works over the intricate chord progression.

The D♭ melodic minor scale will give you some interesting results when played over the C altered dominant chords.

Here's a tasty lick based on an Fm9 arpeggio that works well in this musical atmosphere.

## *Chords for "Slow Ballad"*

V = fret number
x = don't play string

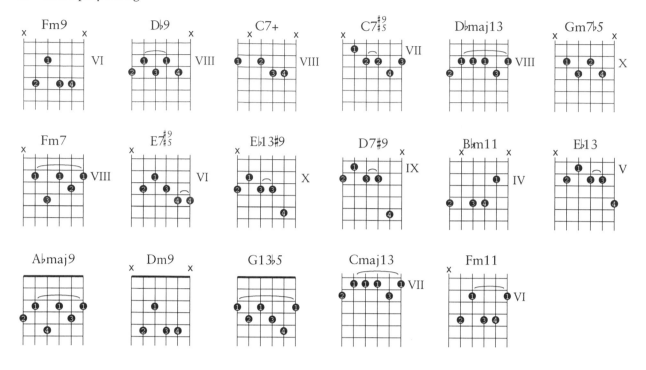

## Slow Ballad

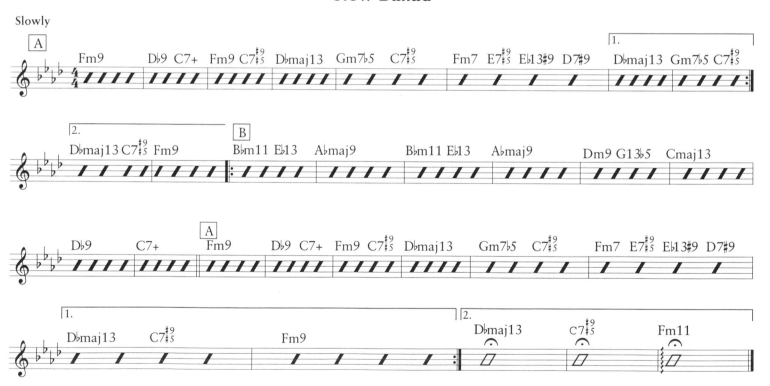